Fireflies

Fireflies
by Joanne Ryder

Pictures by Don Bolognese

A Science I CAN READ Book

Harper & Row, Publishers
New York, Hagerstown, San Francisco, London

FIRST EDITION

Library of Congress Cataloging in Publication Data
Ryder, Joanne.
   Fireflies.

   (An I can read book)
   SUMMARY: Describes the physical characteristics of a firefly from the time it is a glowworm until adulthood.
   I. Bolognese, Don.   II. Title
QL596.L28R93   1977   595.7'64   76-58695
ISBN 0-06-025153-0
ISBN 0-06-025154-9 lib. bdg.

For my aunt, Helen Tischler,

because we have so much in common

In the dark ground,

two pale lights glow.

A male beetle larva is moving.

He looks like a small worm.

But he has tiny lights

under the tip of his belly.

He is called a glowworm.

The glowworm burrows

in the loose, wet earth.

He is hunting for food.

In the darkness

he feels his way

with his antennae.

8

His antennae touch

thin grass roots.

The glowworm squeezes past.

He will not eat the roots.

He does not eat plants.

9

Some loose earth crumbles

underneath the glowworm,

and he falls

into a large mole tunnel.

Bits of earth fall on him.

But he pulls his head

under his hard back.

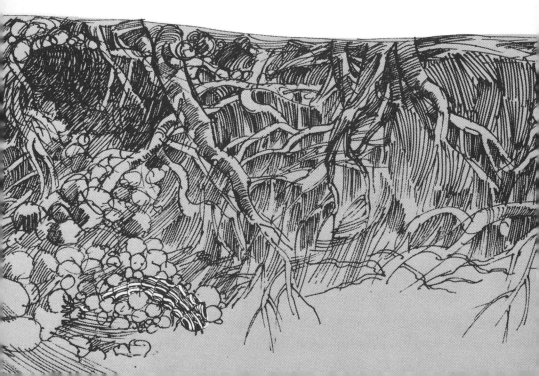

He is not hurt.

His antennae move lightly

over the tunnel floor.

They feel the floor shake.

A mole is coming.

The glowworm finds a small tunnel
and crawls inside it.
The mole is close.
He sniffs.

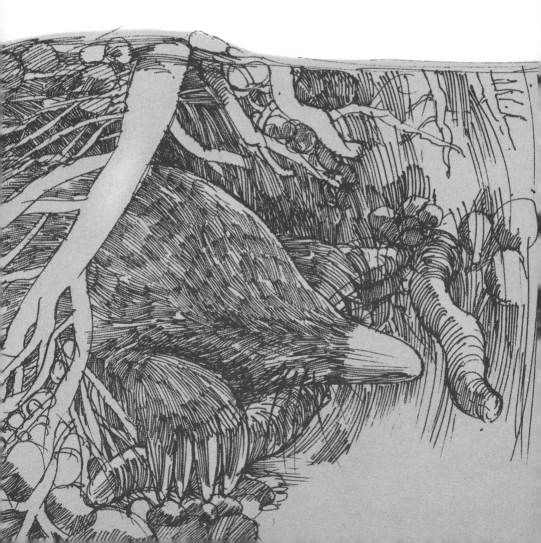

He smells some earthworms.

He stops and eats them.

By then,

the glowworm has crawled away.

The glowworm's antennae

touch something smooth,

something alive.

It is a small earthworm.

Other glowworms

have found it too.

The earthworm tries to escape,

but the glowworms bite it

with their strong jaws.

They bite again and again.

With each bite,

they send poison

into the earthworm's body.

Soon the earthworm cannot move.

The poison makes

the soft body of the earthworm

even softer.

Then the glowworms can eat it.

The glowworm is a full-grown larva.

He has lived underground

for almost two years.

Whenever he grew larger,

he grew a new, large skin

and shed his old, tight one.

In late spring,

the glowworm burrows a bit deeper

in the ground.

In a few days,

he sheds his skin again.

He is now a pupa.

He is pale.

He has weak wings and legs.

As he rests,

his body glows softly.

18

About ten days later,

his skin splits open.

Out crawls an adult beetle.

He has become a firefly.

19

The firefly

cannot live underground.

He crawls up into the air.

It is night.

But it is too late

for the firefly to flash,

and it is rainy.

He will not fly tonight.

The firefly rests

under a dead branch.

His new, long antennae get wet.

He wipes them dry with his legs.

He hides his head

under the shield on his back.

Dark wing cases

protect his wings and belly.

A large part of his belly

is pale yellow.

In it are chemicals

that produce light.

It is a cold light,

a light that does not burn.

The firefly can control his light.

He can flash or not flash.

At dawn, the firefly
crawls through the grass.
His antennae move up and down,
feeling everything.
But now the firefly
can also see his way.

His new, large eyes

see bright colors and light.

The firefly sees something move.

It is an earthworm.

He can now see the worm clearly.

But he turns and crawls away.

He is not looking for food.

He will probably not eat anymore.

The firefly climbs a grass stem.

He is ready to fly.

First he spreads his wing cases.

Then he spreads his wings

and flies into the bushes.

27

During the day,

the firefly hides.

A toad hops under the bush.

zip zip

The toad catches a moth

with his long tongue.

But he does not see the firefly.

The sky darkens.

It is a warm summer evening.

Shortly after sunset,

the firefly crawls out.

He begins slowly flying

across the field.

He begins to flash.

30

The firefly dips

down, then up,

as he flashes his light.

The flash lasts one half second.

It looks like a bright yellow J.

The light is a signal.

Each kind of firefly

flies its own special way

and flashes its own signal.

Soon more fireflies are flashing.

Some dip like the firefly.

Like him, they flash yellow J's.

Others fly very low.

They are another kind of firefly.

They pause over a spot and

flash one very short light.

Their flash looks

like a small bright ball.

All the fireflies flashing

above the field are males.

They are sending signals,

but not to each other.

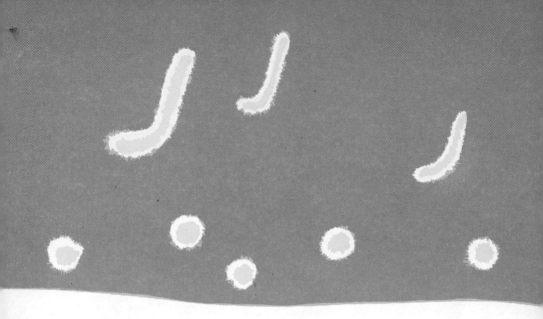

In the grass are female fireflies.

They see the flashing lights

and climb up grass stems.

They wait until

they see the correct signal

from a male of their own kind.

Then they flash too.

The firefly flashes.

So does a low-flying male.

Below, a female flashes right away.

Her short signal comes too quickly.

It is the wrong answer,

and the firefly flies away.

But the low-flying male

flashes again.

The female flashes quickly.

It is the right answer for him.

They are the same kind of firefly.

They will mate.

The firefly sees a group of males
dipping and flashing together.
He flashes with them.
There is a female in the grass.
But another male reaches her first.

The firefly flies past a house.

He sees a male firefly

trapped in a spider's web.

The tiny spider is biting

the firefly's legs.

Her bite is poisonous.

The trapped firefly cannot control

his light anymore.

It glows and glows,

without stopping.

A girl watches the firefly fly near.

He is hard to see

as he flies in the dusk.

But when he flashes,

she can catch him.

The girl feels his antennae

touch her palm.

She sees his flash

light up her fingers.

But his cool light

does not burn her.

The firefly crawls quickly

to the end of her finger

and flies away.

It is growing darker and

the wind begins to blow.

The firefly sees

new fireflies flashing.

They are a different kind.

They begin flying at dusk

and may flash long after it is dark.

They are larger

than many of the early fliers

and their lights are green.

The firefly dips and flashes.

Another male of his kind

dips and flashes too.

Below, a female flashes

her answer.

It is the correct signal.

Both males fly closer.

But the wind catches the firefly
and blows him back.
The other male reaches
the female first.

But she has tricked him.

She will not mate with him.

She is a green-flashing firefly.

She can mimic other females.

She can flash their signals.

And when the male comes,

she eats him.

Only a few bright yellow lights
still flash in the night.
Some of the early fliers have mated.
Others are resting.
They will flash again
another warm evening.
The firefly is still flashing.
But the grass is dark.
He moves on and tries again.

There is a light in the grass!

He sees the long single flash,

and flashes.

Two seconds later,

the female flashes again.

It is the right signal.

He tries to land near the female,

but the wind blows him beyond her.

In the grass,

he flashes.

He raises his antennae.

He stands still and watches.

The female flashes back.

Her light is very small.

But she twists her belly

so her light shines toward him.

54

He turns and crawls toward her.

He flashes again.

He waits for her flash.

She is guiding him to her.

He does not smell her.

He does not hear her.

But he can see her light.

He follows her flashes

until he reaches the stem.

He crawls up.

He touches her with his antennae.

She touches him.

And they mate.

Later the male flies away.

He finds a place to rest.

Like all the fireflies in the field,

he can live only a few weeks more.

His mate stays in the grass.

Her body is full of eggs.

A few nights later,

she begins to lay them

on the ground.

She lays them under grass stems

and among mosses,

one by one.

As each egg develops,

it begins to glow.

A glowworm is forming.

In several weeks,

the little glowworm hatches.

It goes underground.

There it will glow and grow

for two years

until it becomes

a firefly.

Author's Note

There are members of the firefly family on every continent except Antarctica. This book is about one of the most common fireflies in the U.S., *Photinus pyralis*. It is a beetle and has four stages of life: egg, larva, pupa, and adult. It spends its long larval life underground as a glowworm, eating and growing larger. Then it rests briefly as a pupa while its body is changing into the adult firefly.

A firefly flashes when an impulse from its nervous system sets off a chemical reaction within its light organ. These flashes are mating signals. Different kinds of fireflies have different flashing signals.